What's in this book

This book belongs to

_____

你几岁? How old are you?

学习内容 Contents

沟通 Communication

询问年龄
Ask about someone's age

回答年龄
Talk about someone's age

向他人道谢
Thank someone

回应他人道谢
Respond to someone's thanks

背景介绍：
浩浩来到玩具店买玩具，他感兴趣地看着
玩具架上的模型飞机。

生词 New words

★	几岁	how old
★	六岁	six years old
★	他	he, him
★	她	she, her
	我们	we, us
	谢谢	thanks
	不客气	you are welcome

你几岁？   How old are you?

我六岁。   I am six years old.

谢谢。   Thanks.

不客气。   You are welcome.

跨学科学习 Project

制作相簿，并介绍自己
Make a photo album and
introduce yourself

文化 Cultures

中西生日庆祝方式
Birthday celebrations in China
and Western countries

Get ready

参考答案：
1 I visit toy shops every three months.
2 I would choose a football./I do not like the toys here. I like dolls.
3 Hao Hao will choose the model plane/the model rocket.

1 How often do you visit toy shops?

2 What would you choose for yourself from this toy shop?

3 What do you think Hao Hao will choose?

故事大意：
浩浩买了模型飞机，在朋友的帮助下完成了组装。

当别人询问自己的年龄，可以用"我 X 岁。"来回答。

nǐ jǐ suì
你几岁？

我们可以用"你几岁？"来询问别人的年龄。

wǒ liù suì
我六岁。

你几岁？
我六岁。

参考问题和答案：

1 What does Hao Hao buy? (He buys the model plane.)

2 What does '8+' on the packet of the model plane mean? (It means the model plane is for children aged eight and above.)

3 The salesperson wants to know Hao Hao's age. What should she say? ('How old are you?')

4 Hao Hao is telling the salesperson his age. What should he say? ('I am six years old.')

爱莎（Elsa）是浩浩的同班同学，跟浩浩、伊森和艾文同龄。

浩浩、爱莎、伊森和艾文住在同一个社区。
他们在社区的儿童游乐场玩。

我喜欢飞机。

参考问题和答案：

1　Where is Hao Hao? (He is in the playground.)
2　What is he doing? (He is building the model plane.)
3　How does Hao Hao look? (He looks confused.)

你几岁？
我六岁。

参考问题和答案：
Elsa asks about Hao Hao's age. Why do you think she does so?
(Because the model plane is for children aged eight and above. Hao Hao is six years old. She wants to know if it is too difficult for Hao Hao to build it by himself.)

她七岁，我们一起玩。

参考问题和答案：
Is Elsa's friend younger or older than Hao Hao? (She is older than Hao Hao. She is seven years old.)

我们都喜欢飞机。

参考问题和答案：

1 The children are all helping Hao Hao build the model plane. What should Hao Hao say to them? ('Thank
2 What should Elsa say in response to Hao Hao? ('You're welcome!')
3 Do you think that the children will be able to build the model plane? Why? (Yes, because there are five o
   them working together.)

延伸活动：
告诉学生，这个故事传达
的信息是"人多力量大"。
让学生讲讲自己经历过的
或听到过的"人多力量大、
智慧广"的事情。

我们六岁吗？
不，我们八岁。

参考问题和答案：
Why do the children say that they are eight years old? (Because the model plane is for children aged eight and above. Although none of them are eight years old, they managed to build the model plane together. They are smarter as a group.)

Let's think

1 How old is each child? Match the puzzles.

提醒学生根据拼图的缺口找到人物对应的年龄。

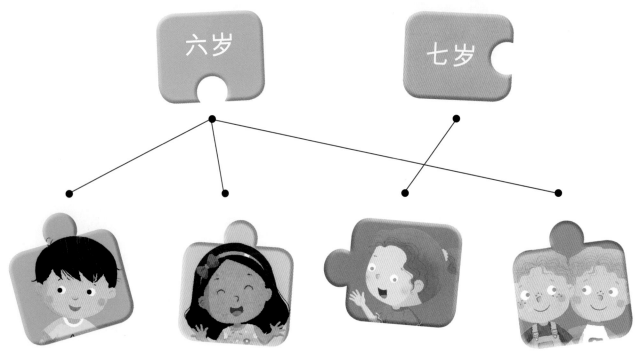

六岁　七岁

2 Which toy is suitable for you? Tick in the box.

提醒学生选择一个年龄范围适合自己，同时最接近自己年龄的玩具。

New words

1 Learn the new words.

谢谢。

不客气。

几岁？

我们

他

她

六岁

2 Match the words to the pictures. Write the letters.

1   a 他   b 她

2   a 你几岁？   b 我六岁。

b

a

a

b

告诉学生中国人用这个手势表示数字"六"。

听听说说 Listen and say

第一题录音稿：
我叫浩浩，我六岁。

1 Listen and tick the correct picture.

四岁 ☐

七岁 ☐

六岁 ✓

2 Look at the pictures. Listen to the sto

第二题参考问题和答案：

1 Ethan wants to play cards with Hao Hao and Esther. Are the cards suitable for their ages? (Yes. The cards are for children aged six and above. Ethan and Hao Hao are six years old. Esther is seven years old. They can play the cards.)
2 What is your favourite toy? (My favourite toy is a toy cat/a robot.)

say.

3 Write the letters. Role-play with your friend.

a 他　b 她　c 几岁

Task

Draw your friend and introduce him/her.

他/她几岁?

他/她叫什么名字?

Game

Listen to your teacher and colour the birds.

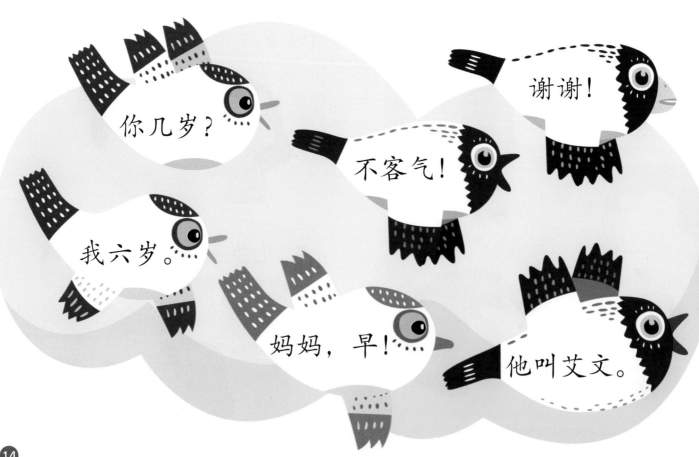

你几岁?

谢谢!

不客气!

我六岁。

妈妈，早!

他叫艾文。

Song

🎧 05 Listen and sing.

我的朋友你几岁？

我六岁呀我六岁。

他们和她们几岁？

他们五岁六岁七岁。

"他们"指自己和对方以外的几个人；
"她们"指自己和对方以外的几个女性。

课堂用语 Classroom language

坐下。
Sit down.

站起来。
Stand up.

举手。
Raise your hand.

写一写 Write

1 Learn and trace the stroke.

老师示范笔画功夫，学生跟着做：坐在地上双腿伸直并拢，两手放在身体两侧。从右侧看过去，身体的形状即为"竖折"的形状。

竖折

2 Learn the component. Trace 山 to complete the characters.

学生观察图片，引导他们发现"山"字的形状像三座连在一起的、中间高两边低的山。

3 Colour 山 to climb the mountain.

4 Trace and write the character.

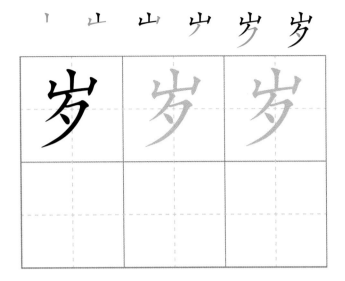

丨 屮 山 少 岁 岁

岁 岁 岁

5 Write and say. 告诉学生 Esther 在询问浩浩的年龄。

你几 岁 ？

我六 岁 。

汉字小常识 Did you know?

Characters are made up of different components and have different structures.

Colour the components in any colour you like.

艾 颗 十 岁 他 牙

复习前面学过的上下、左右结构的汉字和单一结构的独体字。学生小组讨论上方汉字的结构：上下结构——艾、岁；左右结构——颗、他；独体字——十、牙。

Cultures

1 Do you know the different ways to celebrate birthdays?

Birthday celebrations in China

生日快乐

寿桃包和长寿面的寓意
都是健康、长寿；红鸡
蛋代表吉祥喜庆。

birthday bun

birthday eggs

birthday noodles

Birthday celebrations in Western countries

Happy Birthday

Happy BIRTHDAY

birthday cake with candles

延伸活动：
学生说说自己国家的生日庆祝方式。

2 How do you celebrate your birthday? Draw on the right.

Project

1 Make a photo album.

材料：一张彩纸、一把剪刀。

将长方形彩纸上下对折，再展开。

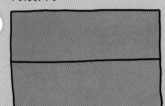

将彩纸左右对折。

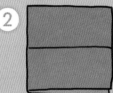

沿开口向两侧拉开。

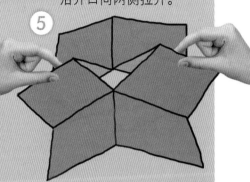

将开口的两边分别沿中线对折。

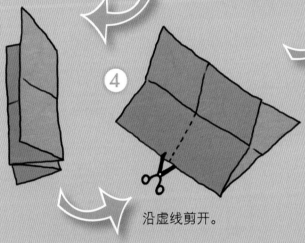

沿虚线剪开。

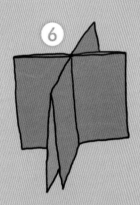

Arrange your photos in order and stick them on the pages.

2 Show the photo album to your friends and talk about yourself.

这是我。
这是一岁的我。
这是两岁的我。
这是三岁的我……

游戏方法：

方法一：学生从"Start"开始，依次正确回答小径上面设
的八道题目，即可帮浩浩找到玩具店。

方法二：学生两人一组，先用橡皮制作简易骰子（两面写
"1"，两面写"2"，最后两面写"3"），然后轮流投掷并在
盘上前进相应步数，再回答停留的方格内的问题。看谁能
快帮浩浩找到玩具店。

1 Help Hao Hao walk from his home to the toy shop.

Finish

Reply to
谢谢 in
Chinese.

不客气!

Say thanks
to Dad in
Chinese.

爸爸，
谢谢!

2 **Work with your friend. Colour the stars and the chillies.**

Words and sentences	说	读	写
几岁	☆	☆	🌶
六岁	☆	☆	☆
他	☆	☆	🌶
她	☆	☆	🌶
我们	☆	🌶	🌶
你几岁？	☆	☆	🌶
我六岁。	☆	☆	🌶
谢谢。	☆	🌶	🌶
不客气。	☆	🌶	🌶

Ask about someone's age	☆
Talk about someone's age	☆
Thank someone	☆
Respond to someone's thanks	☆

3 **What does your teacher say?**

评核建议：

根据学生课堂表现，分别给予"太棒了！(Excellent!)"、"不错！(Good!)"或"继续努力！(Work harder!)"的评价，再让学生圈出上方对应的表情，以记录自己的学习情况。

21

分享 Sharing

Words I remember

几岁	jǐ suì	how old
六岁	liù suì	six years old
他	tā	he, him
她	tā	she, her
我们	wǒ men	we, us
谢谢	xiè xie	thanks
不客气	bù kè qi	you are welcome

延伸活动：
1 学生用手遮盖英文，读中文单词，并思考单词意思；
2 学生用手遮盖中文单词，看着英文说出对应的中文单词；
3 学生三人一组，尽量运用中文单词分角色复述故事。

Other words

喜欢	xǐ huan	to like
飞机	fēi jī	plane
一起	yī qǐ	together
玩	wán	to play
都	dōu	both, all
不	bù	no, not
是	shì	to be

OXFORD

UNIVERSITY PRESS

Oxford University Press is a department of the University of Oxford.
It furthers the University's objective of excellence in research, scholarship,
and education by publishing worldwide. Oxford is a registered trade mark of
Oxford University Press in the UK and in certain other countries

Published in Hong Kong by
Oxford University Press (China) Limited
39th Floor, One Kowloon, 1 Wang Yuen Street, Kowloon Bay,
Hong Kong

© Oxford University Press (China) Limited 2017

Illustrated by Anne Lee and Wildman

Photographs for reproduction permitted by Dreamstime.com

China National Publications Import & Export (Group) Corporation is an authorized distributor of
Oxford Elementary Chinese.

Please contact content@cnpiec.com.cn or 86-10-65856782

ISBN: 978-0-19-942971-4

10 9 8 7 6 5 4 3 2

Teacher's Edition
ISBN: 978-0-19-082150-0

10 9 8 7 6 5 4 3 2